Productivity 20/20

Reshaping the Workplace to Improve Talent Retention

Phyllis Horner, PhD &
Manfred Zapka, PhD

Productivity 20/20 – Reshaping the Workplace to Increase Talent Retention

Copyright: 2020 © Phyllis C. Horner and Manfred J. Zapka, Co-Authors

ISBN# 978-1-941832-07-3

Publisher: Wisdom Media International LLC

Great Places & Spaces™, myPQ™ and WorkPlaceROI™ are active Service Marks.

All rights reserved. No part of this publication may be reproduced, stored in retrieval system, copied in any form or by any means, electronic, mechanical,
photocopying, recording or otherwise transmitted without written permission from the publisher. You must not circulate this book in any format.

This book is licensed for your personal enjoyment only. This Leadership Guide may not be resold or given away to other people without written permission from the authors.

Thank you for respecting the hard work of the authors.

You can also find out more about the authors and upcoming books online at www.greatplacesandspaces.com or contact us at info@greatplacesandspaces.com

PREFACE

The modern workplace is going through dramatic changes. Productivity is down and it's becoming harder and harder to attract and retain top talent, even for well- established companies.

These problems are not completely new. Over our 30 years of experience in business, we have both seen the ever-increasing push to do more with less, gaining results from people without understanding key elements of their personal needs.

One of us (Phyllis), a business psychologist and executive coach, has spent her entire career on "people systems" including performance management, corporate values creation, career and executive coaching, onboarding, succession and employee engagement.

Working to create value through happy, productive people, she created ROI formulas for engagement and learning. She discovered that what was missing was a way to measure and value the worth of individual perceptions – and that turnover was directly related to these perceptions.

Manfred, the Healthy Building Expert, was working in the LEED/WELL and comfort studies world for that same time frame. He discovered that the missing link in building optimization was the ability to measure the personal impact of working conditions.

For example, he found that some building occupants did better with afternoon sun, and others liked it cooler. Traditional comfort studies said that 80% satisfied is enough – yet he knew that we could do better by giving personal choice.

Recently, the research on both sides – the culture and the physical setting – have begun to converge in an explosion of data about the corporate cost of ignoring individual perceptions. The employee experience movement is a new concept which shows that individual points of view do matter to organizational results.

On the physical side, the workplace costs and benefits of individual reactions to noise, light, temperature and other factors has been measured psychologically in a much broader way.

It's time for these two perspectives to converge. By learning each other's point of view and studying the research together, along with our years of experience on the different sides of productivity, we realized that it's time to figure out the connection in a measurable way in order to get better results. Though technology and AI will have an impact, people are still important. We posit a way to move beyond silos to ensure that employees have the culture and the physical environment they personally need to do their best work.

The psychological impact of the physical setting can either enhance or limit the employee work experience. The same is true for the culture — physical responses to the culture abound in stress, burnout and health costs. It's time to address both aspects in a connected way.

This Guide to reshaping the workplace is a different kind of book - meant to inspire, educate, provoke thinking, and suggest easy actions to move toward a successful future.

"Keep away from people who try to belittle your ambitions. Small people always do that, but the really great ones make you feel that you, too, can become great."

Mark Twain

ACKNOWLEDGMENTS

Thanks to our mentors, our clients, our coaches and family.

To our clients who believe in what we stand for and who, through progressive action, lead the way to a better experience of work for all, we thank you for your example.

To our coaches, Ari Iny, Danny Iny, Andy Thompson, Lisa Bloom and our colleagues Rob & Kitty Kooijmans, Jack Roose PhD, Dave Lakhani, Alison Zecha and others, thank you for your honest feedback and for your deep insights.

And to our daughters, Lani and Lena, who deserve workplaces that help them shine, we say "go for it and find a place that lets you do your best work!"

We dedicate this book to the leaders who have the foresight to open their minds about what their workplace needs to be, and who have the curiosity, grit and dedication to make their workplaces warm and welcoming to all who work there.

CONTENTS

Preface i
Acknowledgments vii
Introduction 1
PART 1. Today's Productivity Model Is Broken. 7
PART 2. The Cost Of "Wait And See" 49
PART 3. "Get Off The Fence" To The Future .. 73
PART 4.The New Productivity Roadmap 95
Final Thoughts 123
About The Authors 126

> "Talent attraction and retention are the biggest internal concerns of C-Suite Executives globally."
>
> Conference Board
> C-Suite Challenge 2019

INTRODUCTION

We can all see that the ability to attract, support and retain the best talent is getting harder and harder.

Talking with leaders around the country. from Smart Cities to employers of choice, there is a keen desire to solve this problem.

The 2019 Conference Board's C-Suite Challenge confirmed that talent attraction and retention are the two topics top of mind — what keeps CEO's up at night - for leaders in the private sector.

Modern organizations are building for the future so that they can reap the rewards of ever more sophisticated tools, such as AI.

While technology provides game changing opportunities to increase the bottom line, once ROI is achieved, a motivated and talented workforce is required, to operate the technology and to provide innovative and creative ideas to hold market share against the competition.

The problem is how to simultaneously increase results and productivity without losing engagement or retention.

Introduction

The push for results has caused chronic workplace Issues such as emotional burnout, marginalization and physical ailments. The view that these problems are up to the employee to solve is outdated.

To win the talent war, organizations can no longer make employees responsible to motivate themselves to "fit in" to work settings that don't work for them. Accommodations for physical conditions started the trend. But now, many more accommodations are occurring – for stress reduction, cognitive impairments, weight and other personal conditions.

Employee voice is increasing to the extent that the problems raised no longer can be viewed as "personal". These chronic problems are symptoms of unworkable company systems that need new insight and accountability. And this means that leaders themselves must take responsibility for knowing what works for each person and provide it to the extent possible. Productivity is the central system needing a new look and new measures.

There is overwhelming evidence that the time has come. Numerous books of case studies and productivity models have laid the responsibilities of creating a supportive workplace environment squarely in the lap of leadership. It's not for lack of trying – it's just been unclear about what to do differently. Even investments in open space office layouts have troubles – they look great, but they don't make good work settings for all people to do their best work.

Strategies to create work settings where all employees can do their best work make total sense. Today that means integrate healthy corporate culture AND optimal physical workspaces for all. Companies who adopt this integrated strategy will differentiate themselves vs. being left behind in the dust of old thinking. Quite simply, Space and Place make magic happen.

Luckily, the solution has been hiding in plain sight the entire time... it just didn't seem relevant or measurable before. To understand why, it's important to understand how we got here.

> **"If you are stuck in a hole, stop digging"**
>
> Will Rogers

In the old model of employee productivity, the employee's "hands were tied."

THE SEARCH FOR OPTIMAL PRODUCTIVITY

For decades, workforce productivity improvement has been vigorously pursued. Over 3,000 books on Amazon are currently listed for this topic. The reason? The changing roadmap to productivity keeps being updated like the GPS Maps in your car.

It's a never-ending story, one that started with linking the historical view of productivity to a new match of work setting and expectations.

The historical model of productivity was based on a non-human model, a machine model of efficiency where achieving results that the boss expected was the only measure of success.

And where, if employees didn't measure up, they were stuck — they had to fix their weaknesses no matter what.

Ask yourself a tough question...

      How far away from that model is your company's view today?

"Improved productivity means less human sweat, not more."

Henry Ford

PART 1.
TODAY'S PRODUCTIVITY MODEL IS BROKEN

The way we think of productivity is nearsighted - just like the historical model was years ago, before employee engagement became a key measure.

TOPICS WE'LL DISCUSS IN PART 1

- A seismic shift – the employee experience era
- Why productivity is shrinking & exiting is up
- Physical work settings affect our people more individually than we have assumed
- How three energy draining problems—overwhelm, marginalization and burnout, are limiting wellbeing
- Why employee engagement is like "Calling your Mother"

Does it feel like you're throwing money down the drain when it comes to increasing productivity and retention?

PART I. TODAY'S PRODUCTIVITY MODEL IS BROKEN

LET'S EXPLORE WHY -

Many leaders are frustrated - they feel they have tried many things but have not yet cracked the code on better engagement, retention or well-being of their people.

The broken productivity model of today is costing US businesses more than 1 Trillion dollars annually: $550 Billion in reduced productivity (Gallup, 2015) **plus** $600 Billion in turnover costs (Work Institute Retention Report, 2018).

The uncomfortable truth (Gallup, 2015) is that 2 of every 3 employees are unhappy with the workplace, and they reduce productivity when that happens. According to the Center for Disease Control (2015), costs include:

- Absenteeism - $225B
- Worker's Compensation and Disability - $117B
- Medical Treatment including Stress - $232B

Work overload, a pervasive problem across the country for all job categories, reportedly decreases productivity by 68% for employees who don't have enough time to finish their tasks in a normal day. (Cornerstone, 2015)

Ask yourself a tough question - can you really say that your business doesn't have these problems?

Most of us have to admit we can't, and there is a reason why.

PART I. TODAY'S PRODUCTIVITY MODEL IS BROKEN

HIDDEN PRODUCTIVITY COSTS

It's natural in life and work for everyone to want to feel

> Appreciated
> Comfortable
> Connected
> Understood
> Included
> Fairly Treated
> and Free to make Personal Choices.

Unfortunately, our companies haven't kept pace with what that means as times change. Our view of people is pretty much the same as it was at the beginning of the "knowledge worker" era.

So even though we make serious efforts to ensuring our employees feel satisfied and we even measure this annually, most have to admit that, given the changing statistics about disengagement, something is broken.

What is it?

The Seismic Shift ...

Is your company on the "Fault Line?"

PART I. TODAY'S PRODUCTIVITY MODEL IS BROKEN

THE BEDROCK OF BUSINESS PRODUCTIVITY IS MAKING A SEISMIC SHIFT...

and it's **silently** happening as we speak.

You can likely feel the tension. On one side, employees are expecting better working conditions and more personal control...

...on the flipside is organizations' **reluctance to invest in what employees expect** unless it's warranted and connected to ROI. Leaders feel the need to have control of **workflow, environment and results.**

The gap is widening as employees see work as just another aspect of life, vs. life needing to conform to expectations at work. This gap in perceptions is why the engagement numbers are not moving in many businesses, and why there is increasing stress, burnout, health care costs and loss of talent.

Is there a way to bridge that gap? YES!

   But, it requires looking at things differently.

To succeed, businesses need to "design an organization where people want to show up, by focusing on the cultural, technological and physical environments."

Jacob Morgan,
The Employee Experience Advantage

PART I. TODAY'S PRODUCTIVITY MODEL IS BROKEN

WELCOME TO THE EMPLOYEE EXPERIENCE ERA...

Where the productive environment is defined by **what works for EACH employee.**

The Employee Experience era is new because, rather than defining engagement by what leadership provides for all employees, individuals feel the right to have conditions that respect their unique needs.

"Eighty-four percent of our survey respondents rated Employee Experience important, and 28 percent identified it as one of the three most urgent issues facing their organization in 2019."
Deloitte Insights

FACT: Creating positive employee experience pays off.

"MIT research shows that enterprises with a top-quartile employee experience **achieve twice the innovation, double the customer satisfaction, and 25 percent higher profits than organizations** *with a bottom-quartile employee experience."*

"It's time to realize that people differ in their recipes for success at work and stop serving them "one-size fits all."

Phyllis Horner, PhD

PART I. TODAY'S PRODUCTIVITY MODEL IS BROKEN

People Need Different "Recipes for Success"

As a result, in order to champion the workplace of tomorrow, it is essential for companies to adjust to a new model of productivity. The need for urgent realignment is because the 5 generations in the workforce of today each think about work differently.

The pace of change is accelerating and the competition for talent is increasing exponentially.

That means that new methods are required to close the gap of what the modern workforce needs and what a modern workplace should look like.

Luckily, momentum is building in that direction, through advances in research on individual differences and productivity.

New data explains why productivity is shrinking.

Ignore your employee's individual needs at your own risk ...

PART I. TODAY'S PRODUCTIVITY MODEL IS BROKEN

WHY PRODUCTIVITY IS SHRINKING, AND EXITS ARE UP...

Employer expectations are higher than ever. We're expecting more contributions from each employee to maintain financial success, while at the same time, we are asking for more complex thinking, innovation and creativity.

On the surface asking each person to "do more with less" may sound like the answer to keep your organization competitive and profitable. But that kind of yesterday thinking will hurt you in the long run... because it's not sustainable.

Think about it... at some point, even the best employees hit the maximum they can deliver in a day.

Concerns about overwork and burnout have grown exponentially.

It doesn't take a rocket scientist to understand that people don't perform better when they are overworked and burned out... **they perform worse, while planning their exit strategy.**

"Voluntary turnover is projected to cost U.S. companies more than $600 billion this year. If the voluntary quit rate continues as projected, turnover costs will increase to nearly $680 billion in 2020, a 19% increase from 2017."

Source: Work Institute 2018 Retention Report

Believe it or not, there is a silver lining within these storm clouds.

PART I. TODAY'S PRODUCTIVITY MODEL IS BROKEN

DID YOU KNOW?
MOST TURNOVER IS PREVENTABLE.

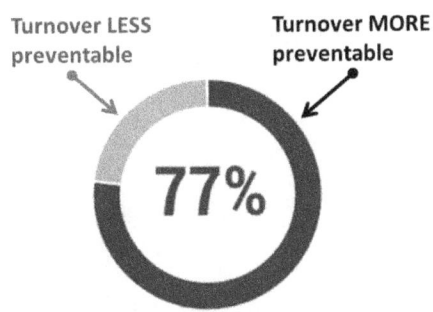

3 of every 4 quits could have been prevented if management knew what the employee wanted and accommodated it. The problem is, many of the employees quitting your company don't give the real reason to the Human Resources representatives. Don't believe that? Check Glassdoor ratings.

As employee expectations and willingness to walk away from organizations have increased, companies have employed various methods to ensure productivity continues. Most of the solutions are individual *"deals"* at the last minute before a talented person walks out the door.

That's a sign to you – **a Yield sign** that can lead to big opportunity for those with eyes to see!

If you pay for a whole pizza, what do you think if you only get 3 or 4 slices?

You've been robbed, right?

Yes, that's what your employees think about your workplace right before they leave you for another employer. You promised them meaningful work and autonomy, but what did they get?

PART I. TODAY'S PRODUCTIVITY MODEL IS BROKEN

If this is making you a bit uncomfortable, that's good... it's a positive thing, because it makes you aware of the problems and sharpens your instincts to find solutions.

And the past data may have failed you in seeing the seismic change as it started to happen:

- You may have few complaints from your talent.

- Your employee engagement scores may be great, 80% satisfied or more overall.

- And your turnover rate may be the same as any other company in your industry.

But what if there is a better way to measure and choose your resource allocation to people and space, without it costing you wasted money? What if you could recoup the hidden cost of disengagement from even 20% of your workforce?

Wouldn't you want to find out?

PART I. TODAY'S PRODUCTIVITY MODEL IS BROKEN

THE UNCOMFORTABLE STATS:

- **2 of every 3 employees are unhappy** with the workplace, and they reduce productivity when that happens, costing businesses up to **$550B per year not including the cost of turnover** (Gallup, 2015).

- **They call in sick** before they leave. Absenteeism costs businesses $225B per year (Center for Disease Control, 2015)

- **They take stress leave** or go on Worker's Compensation and Disability to the tune of $117B

- Or they **seek medical treatment** including anxiety, fatigue, anger and other signs of unhappiness, estimated at $232B

When so many people are unhappy, you have a choice. You can blame them all saying they just don't fit the culture, or have unrealistic expectations, or you can face facts.

The modern workplace of tomorrow will be different and you'll either play the hero if you take steps to fix it, or you will suffer the consequences if you choose to ignore it.

"Two things are infinite: the universe and human stupidity; and I'm not sure about the universe."

Albert Einstein

PART I. TODAY'S PRODUCTIVITY MODEL IS BROKEN

THE HOLE IN THE BUCKET – EMPLOYEE TURNOVER

Here's the rub. Prior to an employee leaving you, his or her productivity is reduced upwards of 35% (Gallup, 2015). If only a few people had less than optimal performance, you might be ok. But employees are disengaged and leaving their jobs at alarming rates, and the reasons for leaving are not what you think.

The Work Institute's 2016 study reported that by 2020, 33% of employees will leave their jobs annually and move on to another opportunity which, they believe, offers better working conditions.

At a conservative cost of 3 month's salary, plus 6 months to hire and train a replacement, the financial cost is huge. It's reported that voluntary turnover alone costs US organizations $600B+ per year.

Read that sentence again and ask yourself a tough question…What is your company's turnover rate?

Now do the math and you'll start to realize the tremendous opportunity at hand.

PART I. TODAY'S PRODUCTIVITY MODEL IS BROKEN

COULD THIS BE YOU?

Paraphrased Quote from a respected leader:

> "I don't want to continue hearing about suggested improvements from the new hires.
>
> I'm sick of hearing about how we should have more flexible schedules, better office environments, and to prevent senior managers from bullying or ignoring them.
>
> They're just crybabies and this isn't a nursery.
>
> If they don't fit, they can leave."

Want to know what happened next?

4 of 6 top new hires left, costing the company almost $1 million in replacement costs.

PART I. TODAY'S PRODUCTIVITY MODEL IS BROKEN

ASK YOURSELF A TOUGH QUESTION:

Does your company or organization think that if people don't fit, they should just leave? If so, maybe meeting employee needs feels too much like coddling.

Why shouldn't employees "pay their dues" like generations past, silently fitting in as they climbed the ranks in their career?

The short answer is... because times have changed, and competitors offer other opportunities.

When statistics show 2 out of every 3 employees are disengaged, overwhelmed or feeling uncomfortable in the workplaces, **it's time to start a new conversation around creating solutions for this systemic problem.**

Because to build the modern workforce of tomorrow, "fit" can no longer be viewed as a one-way street.

This begs the question: **"What new things are employees unhappy about?"**

PART I. TODAY'S PRODUCTIVITY MODEL IS BROKEN

THE MISSING PIECE IS "HIDING IN PLAIN SIGHT"

Physical work settings are much more important than we know, and matter more individually than we have assumed.

The workforce of yesterday was built around siloed solutions... making piecemeal attempts to maintain and improve employee wellbeing and continually trying to make changes to improve retention and productivity.

The primary factor that has led to the decline of productivity and the ability for companies to attract and retain top talent is that the physical environment has been largely ignored in the process.

In order to optimize productivity and win the talent war, we MUST take a multi-faceted approach where both sides of the equation, physical and psychological, are considered in a connected way.

"Productivity growth, however, it occurs, has a disruptive side to it. In the short term, most things that contribute to productivity growth are very painful."

Janet Yellen, Chair, Board of Governors, Federal Reserve System, 2014 -2018

PART I. TODAY'S PRODUCTIVITY MODEL IS BROKEN

THE CONNECTION BETWEEN PHYSICAL SETTINGS AND PSYCHOLOGICAL WELLBEING

If you think about it, it makes sense that a person's response to your physical work setting and their engagement or psychological well-being at work are connected. It's true for you too.

People don't experience work in "slices or silos" – but in a connected, holistic way. It's like two sides of the same coin. A great workstation doesn't fix loud noise or a micromanaging boss, and vice versa. Perceived deficiencies can stack up until a tipping point of dissatisfaction and "intention to leave" occurs.

The importance of physical space is becoming more urgent with the move to open space offices. Without knowing whether your people think the new space is conducive to productivity, you're shooting in the dark.

Ask yourself a tough question -

When you measure work experience today, do you include the perception of physical space with optimal conditions for each person included?

"A major blind spot for business leaders is the confidence that their corporate culture will enable them to maintain high productivity and retention and recruitment of top talent.

However, many companies are ill prepared in this respect and have insular cultures."

A conclusion of the Conference Board,
C-Suite Challenge 2019,
"The Future-Ready Organization"

NEW CULTURE "DEATH-EATERS"

Do you remember Harry Potter? In these amazing books about good and evil, there were monsters called "Death Eaters" that sucked all the joy out of a person's spirit.

Our businesses run the risk of being like this for some of our employees. Physical settings that make people uncomfortable and cultural mismatches are increasing silently, mostly because "doing more with less" has become the norm.

And for those who feel these energy drains, they don't tell you because their needs may be different than others. They think you don't really want to know, and that you'll "pay them back" negatively for speaking up.

The biggest costs between what people need in a work setting and come from

- ✓ **Overwhelm**
- ✓ **Burnout**
- ✓ **and Marginalization.**

The feeling of being overloaded and unproductive

PART I. TODAY'S PRODUCTIVITY MODEL IS BROKEN

OVERWHELMED WITH TOO MUCH WORK

If it's ever happened to you, you realize how hard it is to function at your best when the workload is just impossible. Your employees agree.

Check out this quote from Cornerstone on Demand (2014).

"Work overload, a pervasive problem across the country for all job categories, reportedly decreases productivity by 68% for employees who don't have enough time to finish their tasks in a normal day."

The survey results emphasize how critical it is for organizations to have a better pulse on their workforce, whether it is gaining the right insight, having the right conversations or enabling the right levels of transparency."

Adam Miller, founder and CEO,
Cornerstone OnDemand

PART I. TODAY'S PRODUCTIVITY MODEL IS BROKEN

Burnout – defined by the World Health Organization as a syndrome conceptualized as resulting from chronic workplace stress that has not been successfully managed.

The causes of burnout are not employee frailty or incompetence, but the "insidious problems of overwork, increasing employer expectations, and the rise of the 'hustle culture' making (us) all feel inferior." *Eric Garten, The Employee Experience Advantage, 2017*

Garten notes that leaders must acknowledge their responsibility in causing and fixing this costly problem (an estimated $125 billion to $190 billion a year in healthcare spending in the U.S.), plus the cost of low productivity, high turnover, and the loss of the most capable talent.

Marginalization is observing or experiencing being actively put-down or made to feel inadequate for something the person cannot control. It's a productivity, morale and retention killer.

MARGINALIZATION

69% of employees report they have been or witnessed marginalization at work.

Marginalization is being actively put-down or made to feel inadequate for something the person cannot control, such as age, being new, their gender, how they speak, their experience, ethnicity, looks, or bringing up uncomfortable new ideas.

And this makes the person feel unsafe psychologically because, well, it could happen again, or happen to them.

"60% of employees who feel unsafe psychologically through marginalization or unfair work environment would quit a job as soon as possible at an employer cost of 3-6 months annual pay."

(Ultimate Software, 2016)

PART I. TODAY'S PRODUCTIVITY MODEL IS BROKEN

WHY EMPLOYEE ENGAGEMENT IS LIKE "CALLING YOUR MOTHER"

You only tell her what she's ready to hear.

This is the reason engagement surveys are not enough. Even though you measure many opinions, you are missing some real information.

If you've spent time and money on these surveys, you may wonder how it's possible that you don't know what your employees want. After all, don't you show you're serious, setting action plans and tracking progress?

One problem is that those surveys make assumptions about what all people want to be satisfied.

And they lead to group solutions, but it's individuals who leave. Treating these responses like the full recipe for success is like saying fast food is equal to fine dining.

There are unique individuals across 5 generations in our companies, so it makes sense that what works for one person may not for another.

PART I. TODAY'S PRODUCTIVITY MODEL IS BROKEN

ARE YOU UNCONSCIOUSLY USING OLD ASSUMPTIONS TO SOLVE TODAY'S PROBLEMS?

If you said yes or maybe, there is huge opportunity once you start to consider approaching the physical and cultural work setting in an interconnected way.

Because approaching the issues of psychological and physical workplace settings in a compartmentalized fashion won't help you fix the problem.

PART I. TODAY'S PRODUCTIVITY MODEL IS BROKEN

LET'S RECAP

To optimize the productivity of each employee and be able to attract and retain the very best talent. Here are three ideas worth remembering:

- Employees need time and freedom, in various work settings, to deliver creativity and innovation which you expect from them.

- We need to eliminate any disconnect between the work life balance implied at hire, and the subsequent push for more results in less time.

- Each person has personal "ideal productivity conditions" and when these are not met, even if you think everything is fine, many become disengaged, reducing their productivity, and are more likely to leave.

PART I. TODAY'S PRODUCTIVITY MODEL IS BROKEN

Time for Action! Here's how to start solving for ideal productivity.

1. Take a good look at your physical workspaces. Look for people with sweaters, headphones, squinting, looking down. Feel the airflow and temperature as you go from one space to another. Wonder what it feels like to be working in these conditions.

2. Do some research. Keyword search "sick building syndrome and stress from open offices". Don't delegate this to HR or to your exec assistant. Consider what you find.

3. Ask to see the budget (or pull it up onscreen) for the physical layout, office furnishings and air quality of your various offices. Add this to the budget for employee surveys and supervisory training and development. Consider the combined costs and the results you are getting.

4. Refresh your knowledge about turnover in your organization (don't delegate this either). Estimate how much the loss of talent is costing you annually (use 2x annual salary for each professional level quit). Note the annual amount from last year.

ASK YOURSELF THESE TOUGH QUESTIONS

- What insights did this data gathering provide me?
- Who else needs to go through this exercise as well?
- Why do we solve the physical and culture problems as if they aren't connected?

What if there were ways to gain a better view about the impact for your company?

ND THEN WHAT?

PART 2.
THE COST OF "WAIT AND SEE"

Topics We'll Discuss in Part 2

- Costs of "Wait and See"
- The Financial and Productivity Costs of
    - ✓ Unhealthy Physical Work Settings
    - ✓ Culture Deficiencies
- What You Can Expect if Your Company Gets Left Behind

HOW TO CONNECT INITIATIVES FOR A MORE EFFECTIVE SYSTEM

HOW TO KNOW WHEN TO TAKE NEW ACTION

Most leaders today are trying to meet their employees half-way – to ensure they feel like they have career potential, can make a difference and even enjoy coming to work.

A great deal of money is invested to achieve these results and keep the talent attraction, productivity and retention machine going. You've likely done engagement strategies, team events, values and invested in stand-up desks and others. But you've just as likely been approaching things in a compartmentalized fashion.

After the surveys and assessments and action plans, and physical improvements, the results are mixed. Some people are happier, others don't say, and the workplace is still not optimized.

We talked about what's missing from a great workplace in Part 1. In this section we quantify what happens if you just choose a "slow" path to change - and allow competitors to take these actions first.

What harm could that do to your business?

We'll help you discover the financial cost of playing "wait-and-see."

"The secret to happy workplaces isn't spending more money. It's about creating the conditions that allow employees to do their best work."

Ron Friedman,
The Best Place to Work: The Art and Science
of Creating an Extraordinary Workplace, 2014

PART 2. THE COST OF "WAIT AND SEE"

Ensuring productivity today can no longer be a top-down situation. You need to ask each person what they need to be productive.

So, what kind of problems is an organization likely to face if they resist bridging this gap and making these changes?

The data shows that financially, it is like leaving money on the table!

Physical setting comfort and productivity-friendly settings as well as healthy cultural practices need to be addressed together, in order to increase productivity and compete favorably in the talent war.

PART 2. THE COST OF "WAIT AND SEE"

COSTS OF WAIT AND SEE

Employees who perceive their company as tone-deaf to what they need to be productive, will perform poorly and have increased health problems.

Michael Bush's 2017 book *"A Great Place to Work for All: Better for Business, Better for People, Better for the World"* describes the inequities for several employee groups, and clarifies that companies need to value their employees' interests and priorities to be successful.

Even in best places to work, the workplace does not work equally well for all employees.

The next few pages describe selected costs you can expect.

PART 2. THE COST OF "WAIT AND SEE"

COSTS OF INACTION – EMPLOYEES WILL "VOTE WITH THEIR FEET"

1. Employees today have more opportunities and are more fearless in choosing their place of work than before. Even if a recession occurs, "the genie is out of the bottle" and future workers are more ready to leave the current job for a better job offer.

2. The demand for employees is already outpacing the supply.

3. Older workers are exiting, and the younger workforce is delaying entering the workforce. Those who arrive are not "loyal" as in the past.

4. It's time to acknowledge that **what employees define as their personal optimal conditions for productivity,** is the new normal, and the most accurate productivity barometer we have.

PART 2. THE COST OF "WAIT AND SEE"

Distracting noise can lower performance by up to 66%.

Lawrence Berkeley National Laboratory, Indoor Environment Department, 2017

In addition, Workers can be up to 66% less productive when exposed to just one nearby conversation. Julian Treasure, Chairman of the Sound Agency, 2013

66% less productive means more errors, more distraction, less volume of work, and less innovation.

THE COST OF UNHEALTHY PHYSICAL WORKSPACES

70% of offices are now open plan layouts. Think of how much productivity is being negatively affected, unless you have sound masking to mitigate noise. And there are many other costs in the physical space, as we will see.

Data from the Harvard Healthy Building Program, World Green Building Council and the Lawrence Berkeley National Laboratory shows that **productivity levels depend on the physical workplace's impact on an individual's ability to focus** and reduce harmful conditions.

It is flawed and costly to act as though all is fine with our current policies and systems, and that problems are caused by "problem" employees.

The state of the physical workplace can exacerbate harmful aspects of the corporate culture.

PART 2. THE COST OF "WAIT AND SEE"

THE COST OF NOT CARING ABOUT WHAT EMPLOYEES NEED

Measuring the unanticipated consequences of physical improvements (e.g. new AC systems or open layouts) is essential to maximize productivity for all employees. Do you agree?

Estimates of gains in revenues:

Deficient space settings should be improved to reap additional revenues. These conditions have been identified as causing significant and measurable reductions in vital performance parameters.

PART 2. THE COST OF "WAIT AND SEE"

LET'S ESTIMATE THE DOLLARS LOST

The following five examples show the productivity value of improved physical work conditions.

To estimate, we're assuming a 100-person company with average loaded salaries (including benefits) of $100,000 each.

By improving specific working conditions, you can increase the following financial gains, and mitigate current productivity problems **(annual value per person).**

Lighting: By thoroughly improving deficient artificial light and providing ample daylight: $4,800.

Ventilation: By providing much more than the code required fresh air to the spaces: $6,500.

Indoor air quality: By significantly curbing sources of harmful compounds: $4,400.

Noise: By curbing internal and external noise sources: $6,300.

Views and Biophilia: By providing external views and natural elements, such as plants: $3,300.

"… a leader's job is not to build greatness into people, but instead to acknowledge that greatness already exists… and to devote energy toward creating an environment where greatness can emerge."

Brad Smith, Chairman and CEO of Intuit

PART 2. THE COST OF "WAIT AND SEE"

THE COST OF CULTURE DEFICIENCIES

We know that optimal productivity comes when all employees feel trusted, included (not marginalized), mentored, supported when mistakes occur, given opportunities to grow, and not overworked or micromanaged.

As senior leaders, you may have policies and training courses to ensure good management practices. But experience shows that there are many cultural blind spots (Conference Board, 2019) in ensuring a great culture, and these blind spots can exist even in "great" companies.

As executives, you may think things are optimal in your culture when, in fact, they are not great for all people. For example, a well-known successful tech company in Silicon Valley had inclusion training and diversity initiatives for years before the walkout on unequal treatment of women occurred in 2018. Though leadership thought they did all they needed to, in practice it wasn't enough.

They were caught in a costly blind spot.

"Employees rate their employers on Best Places to Work (BPTW) lists highly, **despite the relentless work demands that take a toll on their health, happiness and family life,** and that affects their morale and their ability to think creatively and reflectively."

Tony Schwartz, "Why the Best Places to Work, Often Aren't", New York Times, 2014

PART 2. THE COST OF "WAIT AND SEE"

People don't reveal their dissatisfaction with the workplace if the stakes are high, such as fear of retaliation or being "bumped" from the promotion list.

Consider these questions:

- Why would employees rate their employer as a Best Place to Work even when they are not thriving in that workplace?

  In statistical terms this is called a "false positive", and the data looks better than the reality.

- What does that mean for companies that rely on the survey results for action plans, management bonuses, and a sense that they are doing everything right?

- What does the mismatch in information cost your company?

"The people who get on in this world are the people who get up and look for circumstances they want and if they can't find them, make them."

George Bernard Shaw

PART 2. THE COST OF "WAIT AND SEE"

MORE EXAMPLES - COSTS OF CULTURE DEFICIENCIES

The cost of cultural deficiencies is huge. These studies show that the financial risk of inaction is high.

- Stress results in calling in sick, which costs employers an average of $602 per employee per year. Harvard Business Review, 2017

- 40% of workers say their jobs are very stressful, and their health care costs are 46% higher than non-stressed employees. SHRM, 2018

- Employees coming in not ready to work because of sleepless nights or overwork costs $ 150 B per year in lost productivity Eastern Kentucky University Occupational Safety Program

- 60% of 25,000 surveyed US Workers would prefer to choose a new career altogether.

- Overall, poor cultures cost companies an estimate of $ 30,000 per year per stressed or marginalized employee – estimated at 60% of the workforce. Mental Health America, 2016

> "The secret of getting ahead is getting started."
>
> Mark Twain

WHAT TO DO TO GET STARTED

The new reality of workplace culture is this:

To keep employees productive, engaged and likely to stay, you need to start doing a few things better:

- Ask individuals what they want in a work setting to feel productive and supported, and how your workplace stacks up

- Update policies that "look good on paper" but are out-of-date or unintentionally marginalize some teammates.

- Use input from employees to update your practices and show action.

With every passing day you don't consider these actions, it costs unforeseen reductions in productivity and retention, and leads to increases in the cost of doing business.

A recent study by Glassdoor indicates that *more than half of employees believed that if they left their jobs, they could easily get a better one within 6 months.*

Summarizing the Impacts and Costs:

- Compromised retention and recruitment of top talent to stay competitive
- Increased absenteeism
- Loss of productivity
- Increased cost for onboarding, recruitment and bringing employees up to speed
- Impacted medical and healthcare costs.
- Inability to innovate and create complex solutions to new challenges
- Reduction in task efficiency & increase in missed deadlines

You are at a crossroads, and it's time to see...

... how companies who figure out what all employees want in a workplace, and offer that, will win the talent war, while those who don't, will be left behind.

SUMMARY

It's time to stop waiting for employees to prove they have good reasons for what they expect from their work settings. This lack of trust of employees reduces productivity and engagement, and increases the risk of healthcare and other costs.

TIME FOR ACTION

1. Ask yourself – What is your personal optimal work setting, physical and otherwise? What are your preferences, and what drives you crazy? Now, imagine the how others would answer the question.

2. Research best in class companies in your industry whose brand is more progressive in the culture or physical space. Consider how those practices affect talent attraction.

3. Ask yourself – What insights did this data gathering provide me?

A growing percentage of your workforce has new work ethics, life priorities and willingness to move on. This "voice of change" is transforming company practices and norms. **The time to act is now.**

Next, we look at how to move forward.

"Success is not final; failure is not fatal: it is the courage to continue that counts."

Winston Churchill

PART 3.
"Get Off the Fence" to the Future

Topics We'll Discuss in Part 3

- Path to Future Preferred Employer
- Is your Business Ready?
- What Does it Take to Succeed?
- The Payoff – Productive Settings.

PART 3. "GET OFF THE FENCE" TO THE FUTURE

> "You can't get much done in life if you only work on days when you feel good."
>
> Jerry West

To succeed in creating the workforce and workplace of the future, the major first step is to learn to listen and adapt to the variety of working conditions that individual employees need to be most productive.

Just like when you listen to your customers' preferences and needs, this step makes you proactive and poised for success with employees.

PART 3. "GET OFF THE FENCE" TO THE FUTURE

PATH TO FUTURE PREFERRED EMPLOYER

Here's the missing link: Companies that make the shift to a new productivity model that combines the physical and psychological elements will be the preferred employers in the future. What will they enjoy?

- Knowing what their people want from the physical setting and from the culture – **a unique workplace fingerprint.**

- Resilience and flexibility to provide needs as they emerge with new generations.

- Assurance that most of their employees will agree with physical or cultural changes they propose.

- A way to position themselves as ready for what next-gen employees will need and expect.

- Measurable ROI on their efforts and actions.

So, where do you go from here... and how can you see payoffs quickly? Let's figure out if your business is ready.

PART 3. "GET OFF THE FENCE" TO THE FUTURE

Which side of the future are you on?

It's time to choose, because the race to meet employee expectations has already begun and it's picking up steam very quickly. If you are on the wrong side, it may be too late – like betting on Beta over VHS, Blockbuster over Netflix.

Things simply move too fast these days to be on the wrong side of innovation.

PART 3. "GET OFF THE FENCE" TO THE FUTURE

STILL ON THE "FENCE" TO THE FUTURE?

You may be worried because, after all, how could you possibly meet every employee's unique view of what they need to be productive?

You may be thinking, *"I already ask how employees view some of these important areas. What's the difference?"* **The difference is to ask specifically what each person needs for full productivity vs. what they think they are getting with your firm.**

You may worry – I'm just stirring up expectations. What if I can't provide what people want?

REMEMBER, YOU GOT THIS!

Look at it this way. You are likely already losing very talented people and we know that with inaction, you will likely continue to lose people to your competitors who learn to listen to individual needs.

And, guess what... you don't need to be perfect or do everything at once.

Listening, prioritizing, and strategically implementing what is most important to as many employees as possible, is the key to success. But where do you start?

PART 3. "GET OFF THE FENCE" TO THE FUTURE

IS YOUR BUSINESS READY?

Companies that are ready to measure and ensure productivity in the modern workplace see that continuing to do business the traditional way is *"risky business."* They know that measuring what employees specifically need to be productive - and providing that, makes good business sense. They know the secret — that it's the only way to succeed in the talent wars, because they understand that employee working conditions drive productivity as much as their talent does.

> "You just can't beat the person who never gives up."
>
> Babe Ruth

PART 3. "GET OFF THE FENCE" TO THE FUTURE

TAKE THE SHORT 4-QUESTION QUIZ BELOW TO SEE HOW YOU RATE

1. An employee is most productive when he/she works remotely on projects. You just invested in an open workspace and took away remote working. Do you still let him/her do it?	Yes	No	Probably Not
2. You just upgraded the chiller for your AC, and now several departments are 2 degrees colder than they were before. Do you ask employees in those departments if the new temperature gets in the way of productivity?	Yes	No	Probably Not
3. Your new floor plan has a "meditation/relaxation room" that few are using. Do you do a confidential survey to find out why, and how it links to productivity for those who use it?	Yes	No	Probably Not
4. Employees feel overwhelmed because you set additional performance targets too frequently and email them at night. They haven't told you and you haven't asked. If you found out they felt this way, would you change your policies?	Yes	No	Probably Not

PART 3. "GET OFF THE FENCE" TO THE FUTURE

Your Results: If you answered mostly **"Yes"** you are moving toward the new model of productivity. If not, then you are still looking at your employees traditionally, no matter how much money you are spending on their well-being.

Even if you answered **"No", you can learn and use new measurement tools easily and be well on your way to greatly reducing human and financial costs.**

PART 3. "GET OFF THE FENCE" TO THE FUTURE

WHAT DOES IT TAKE TO SUCCEED?

To succeed in productivity, attraction and retention, you need three things:

1. A new viewpoint that gets you excited about finding out what individuals think and then matching their needs to your practices. This change may feel hard but is completely under your control.

2. A baseline of how you compete today compared with what employees want and need to do their best work for you. And,

3. New measurement and decision tools that connect the physical and psychological experience of work, and clarify what settings best ensure you get focus, creative thinking and innovation you expect.

These new measures include:

- A way to measure what employees really need in their work settings to be productive.

- A gap analysis measure of what is missing in the work environment.

- A strategic decision tool for senior leaders to prioritize and gain ROI from the improvements they make to close the gap.

PART 3. "GET OFF THE FENCE" TO THE FUTURE

As a successful business, when you make smarter decisions than your competitors about which investment improves productivity for most employees, you'll know that you're satisfying a thirst for what people really need.

> "…in a sense, employee experience is not a program. It's a topic, or maybe a mindset."
>
> Josh Bersin, Bersin by Deloitte, 2019

PART 3. "GET OFF THE FENCE" TO THE FUTURE

THE PAYOFF OF PRODUCTIVE SETTINGS

As Dr. Ron Friedman, author of *The Best Place to Work* said, *"the combination of physical place and culture can amp up engagement, compared with a focus on culture alone."*

The payoff is to be ready for the world described by Jacob Morgan, author of *The Employee Experience Advantage*, who said, *"employees should demand to work for an organization that has been redesigned to truly know its people...and masters the art and science of creating a place where people want to, not need to, show up."*

And, you'll have moved past the limits of engagement and culture surveys. You'll have an integrated view of the workplace and what to do to make it match today's needs.

Adopting this new multi-faceted productivity approach puts you in a powerful position to lead innovation and gain market share.

"Obstacles are those frightful things you see when you take your eyes off your goal."

Henry Ford

PART 3. "GET OFF THE FENCE" TO THE FUTURE

THE FINANCIAL BENEFITS OF IMPROVED PHYSICAL SETTINGS

- Estimated U.S. savings and productivity gains from improved indoor environments of **up to $150 billion / year** Harvard Healthy Building Program
- Workers in green-certified buildings **scored 26.4 percent higher on cognitive tasks** than those in regular buildings. They also had 30 percent fewer "sick building" symptoms: fewer headaches and respiratory complaints, for example.
- Design of an office can **reduce the absenteeism rate of 3% per employee - private sector, and 4% - public sector,** with inaction costing employers $2,074 and $2,502 per employee per year respectively. Source: World Green Building Council
- The **total absence rate was 34% lower** in buildings with high ventilation. Lawrence Berkeley National Laboratory, Indoor Environment Department
- Common **respiratory sickness could be drastically reduced (as much as 70%)** with ample outdoor air supply and advanced filtering of airflow.

"You don't need a
new plan for next year.
You need a commitment."

Seth Godin

PART 3. "GET OFF THE FENCE" TO THE FUTURE

THE LEADERSHIP BENEFITS

Once you commit to start providing physically and psychologically healthy and comfortable work settings, you're on your way to reducing the cost of overwhelm, burnout and stress on health premiums.

But know this: you may feel like It's like situational leadership on steroids. In the past, when subgroups of employees wanted different things from our norms, we would call it a "fit issue", a problem for the employee. Right now, it's clear that it is our leadership problem as well as opportunity.

And the good news is - *it is no more costly than your current productivity and engagement investments.* Why? Because you can reallocate money you already spend better, once you know what employees need...

Successful businesses will no longer rely on what employee engagement experts say employees want in groups, like departments or units. Employees interpret what is too hot or cold, too noisy, Individuals will feel heard and supported, and your ROI can be predicted. Everyone wins.

"Each person's maximum productivity is the product of their ideal physical and psychological experiences of the work setting."

Manfred Zapka, PhD

PART 3. "GET OFF THE FENCE" TO THE FUTURE

THE ULTIMATE PAYOFF – IMPROVED PRODUCTIVITY

Making changes that support employee input allows three positive results: higher complex thinking, creativity, innovation and collaboration. An example of this type of model is high tech, where the workplace design matched the business needs - creativity, and quick results.

It's obvious that when working conditions adjust to ensure they are right for the employee performance instead of blaming employees for systemic failures, a business can attract and retain the best talent compared with competitors who operate "*the old way.*"

The idea of the system working for employees began with W. Edwards Deming, who noted that problems in achieving results was 95% or more because of systems problems, not *"people problems."*

We have made progress, but we still have more to do.

"When employees aren't as productive as they could be, it's usually the organization, not its employees, that is to blame."

Eric Garten - Harvard Business Review, 2017

PART 3. "GET OFF THE FENCE" TO THE FUTURE

WAIT! WHAT ABOUT PERFORMANCE SYSTEMS?

Recently, with the rise of the popular idea of eliminating traditional performance reviews, the tide has turned. **Without SMART goals and numerical ratings, the system of "control" over employee behavior has hit a huge fault line.**

And the new productivity model described in Part 4 is the positive path forward.

PART 3. "GET OFF THE FENCE" TO THE FUTURE

SUMMARY

To succeed as a leader in the future, you need three things – **a new mindset** about what employees deserve and need to do their best work for you, **a baseline** of how well you meet those needs today, and **measurement and decision tools** that are focused on the combined physical and psychological response to working conditions.

TIME FOR ACTION

1. Think about your openness to requests for working arrangements that differ from the norm. If you respond "no", what does this show the employee, and the workforce?

2. Consider what it would mean to ask employees to suggest which work "goes away" as new work gets added. What part of this idea could you see adopting?

3. Ask yourself – What do I imagine would be the benefits of adopting the new connected productivity model in my company?

How can I move forward?

PART 4.
THE NEW PRODUCTIVITY ROADMAP

Getting a more productive workplace that listens better to the needs of individuals is possible without spending more money than you are likely currently spending.

In this section we describe the roadmap to get those results.

Topics We'll Discuss in Part 4

- Fingerprints – Space and Place
- Roadmap to Optimal Productivity
- Two Powerful Solutions
- A Gift

PART 4. THE NEW PRODUCTIVITY ROADMAP

"FINGERPRINTS" OF SPACE AND PLACE

What solutions can you access to help utilize an individual approach to productivity and measurement, while ensuring a positive ROI on your efforts?

Great question! To figure out the best solution for your workforce, it's best to view personal productivity like a fingerprint.

Each person has a unique combination of ideal working conditions which make him / her most satisfied and productive:

- Some need quiet environments with natural light to feel most productive.
- Others like open layouts and lots of background noise.
- Some are open to stern feedback.
- Others have huge productivity dips given the same feedback.
- Some are overwhelmed by the work expectations you set.
- Others experience unconscious bias and marginalization.

Significant differences like these exist in other cultural and physical elements of work.

This can feel overwhelming, but it isn't.

"The way to get started is to quit talking and begin doing."

Walt Disney

THE NEW PRODUCTIVITY ROADMAP

The new productivity roadmap measures the interaction of physical and psychological responses of your employees to their work settings. How is this valuable?

In addition to what is asked in engagement surveys, the new roadmap measures three things of immense value.

1. It **connects the dots** between these physical space and cultural place, and maps interactions. It removes the blind spot that existed when we assumed everyone was the same, and accepts that the physical environment affects a person's response to the culture, and vice versa.

2. The new roadmap **takes a predictive cost approach** to knowing what investments will best pay off for the organization – so the investment will not end up in a "black hole."

3. And, the new roadmap **includes employees in the future planning** so that they have personal choice in ensuring their best work gets done on your behalf.

"You miss 100% of the shots you don't take."

Wayne Gretzky

GETTING PAST SILOS

The result of taking **a "siloed" approach** to work settings leads **to real problems** like these:

- A beautiful new office building where people feel monitored and controlled.
- A great inclusion policy which inadvertently excludes new employees from access to team building
- Absenteeism caused by sensitivity to the prevailing temperature or airflow.
- Headaches from lighting sensitivity reduce personal ability to think, leading to poor performance ratings.
- A meaningful job is great except that the workspace is musty and dark, affecting productivity.
- Office to cubicle transitions where the goal to make everyone equal just makes everyone unhappy and cramped.

Obviously, the leaders of these organizations would never consciously invest in something better to end up with new problems.

What if they had a way to prevent these problems?

PART 4. THE NEW PRODUCTIVITY ROADMAP

TWO POWERFUL SOLUTIONS

Our company mission is to create better work settings, providing tools and assessments to measure the perception of space and place at the individual level, to help companies increase productivity and attract talent.

We have designed a groundbreaking tool to help systemically measure this "crossover" influence in work settings, and another to decide which improvements make the most sense. We'll describe them for you, but first...

Let's look at a model that connects the dots.

There are two aspects of the physical workspace that affect employees :

The physiological responses:

- Adverse conditions at the workspace can make occupants literally physically sick, from bad indoor pollutants borne by bad air, water, noise, lights, smells, etc.

The psychological responses:

- A physical shape and layout of the workspace that lacks a sense of place and welcome can have a powerful negative psychological effect.

Only **a healthy employee** can perform at his/her full potential.

PART 4. THE NEW PRODUCTIVITY ROADMAP

This graphic illustrates how the physical workspace affects employees and their ability to perform their work function productivity and personal wellbeing.

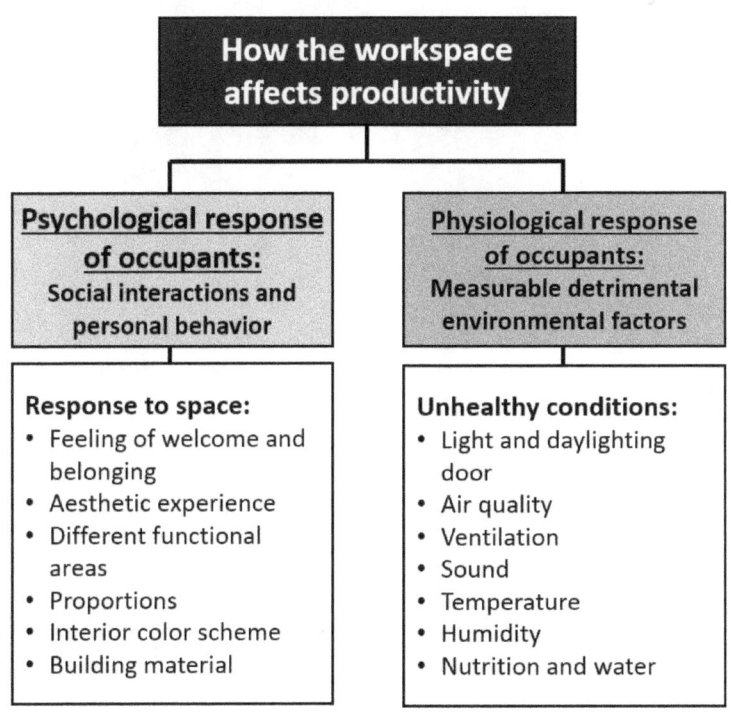

Spaces affect occupants and their ability to perform.

PART 4. THE NEW PRODUCTIVITY ROADMAP

TWO NEW GROUNDBREAKING TOOLS TO GIVE YOU A DISTINCT ADVANTAGE

We have developed two software tools which help employees and companies to identify both psychological and physical workplace conditions which hamper performance and wellbeing.

MyPQ™ is a confidential, individual assessment that indicates which workplace conditions lead to optimal productivity – a personal productivity quotient. It also clarifies which conditions cause a drop in productivity for that person. MyPQ™ indicates if the workplace and the employee needs are a good match and what could be improved.

Take complimentary myPQ™ assessment by visiting our website at

https://greatplacesandspaces.com/myPQ

The ability to calculate the ROI of investments in workplace improvements is a powerful decision tool for leadership to make smart investments.

PART 4. THE NEW PRODUCTIVITY ROADMAP

WorkPlaceROI™ is an assessment software tool to leadership to identify which investments in workplace improvements offer the highest ROI. WorkPlaceROI™ assesses the relative costs and predicted increases in revenues when deficient workplace problems are fixed. WorkPlaceROI™ is a powerful decision tool for leadership to make smart investments.

This powerful new decision tool gives you the ability to affix real dollars to lost productivity caused by specific workspace conditions, and to quickly and accurately assess the ROI of improvement measures.

PART 4. THE NEW PRODUCTIVITY ROADMAP

CAPTURE FINANCIAL BENEFITS FOR YOUR ORGANIZATION

Using these tools and others, it is now possible to:

- **Honestly assess** where you are in both physical and psychological productivity,

- **Measure the reduced productivity** that is invisibly affecting your bottom line,

- **And, determine which priority actions** will have the biggest payoff for your company.

PART 4. THE NEW PRODUCTIVITY ROADMAP

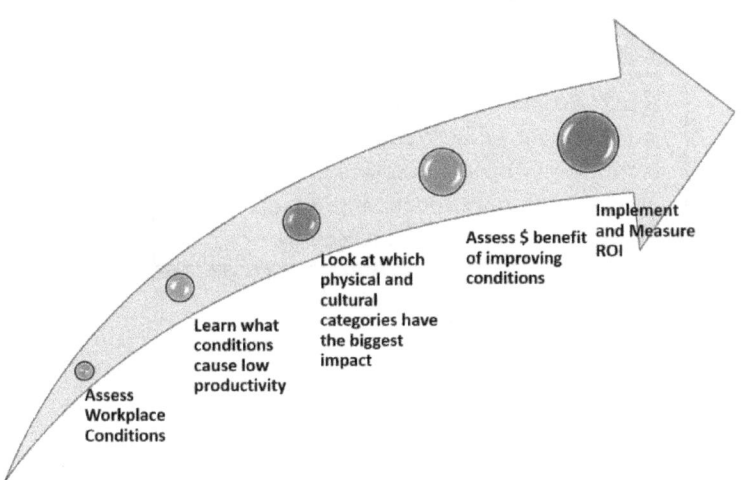

This model illustrates how we work with business leaders to determine which physical or cultural initiatives are likely to have the best payoff.

PART 4. THE NEW PRODUCTIVITY ROADMAP

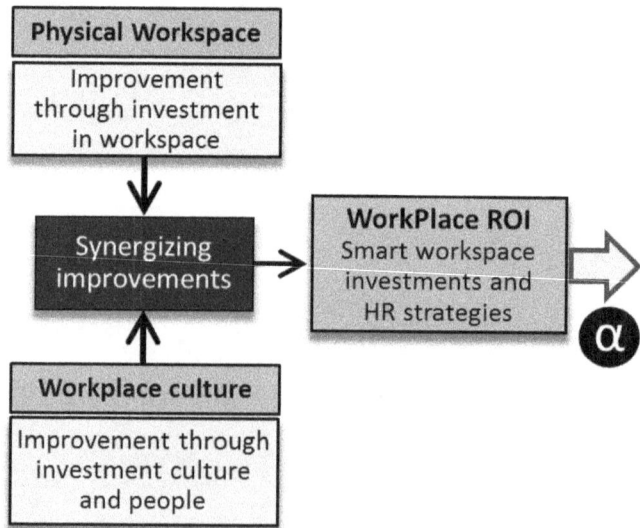

PART 4. THE NEW PRODUCTIVITY ROADMAP

Target: Quantify & decide which investments pay off most
- Improve productivity and engagement
- Lower health related risks and absenteeism
- Higher retention rates / less turnover cost
- Improve ability to attract and hire essential talent

Solves both parts of problem
Best cost vs. Benefit

Winning Formula: Organizations that provide productive and healthy workplace and engaging workplace culture have competitive advantage, fewer productivity losses and reduced risks in the people space

PART 4. THE NEW PRODUCTIVITY ROADMAP

Workplace ROI

Quadrant 1 – "Let's Get Out of Here!" is where employees who are mobile seek to leave the organization because of a less than healthy physical workplace and/or an unproductive culture.

Quadrant 2 – "Gilded Cage" Employers who score in this quadrant are characterized by beautiful surroundings, modern layouts, pristine air and water. However, they are less effective in creating a healthy culture.

Quadrant 3 – "Rose Colored Glasses" Employers who score in this quadrant have created a positive workplace culture. They are weaker on the physical aspects of productivity.

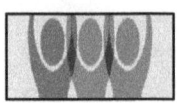

Quadrant 4 – "This is THE Place!" Employers who score in this quadrant have made a strong workplace, both on the physical productivity side, as well as the socio-emotional productivity side. They likely have less turnover of high talent and have a highly productive work environment.

OUR ROADMAP FOR OPTIMIZING THE WORKPLACE

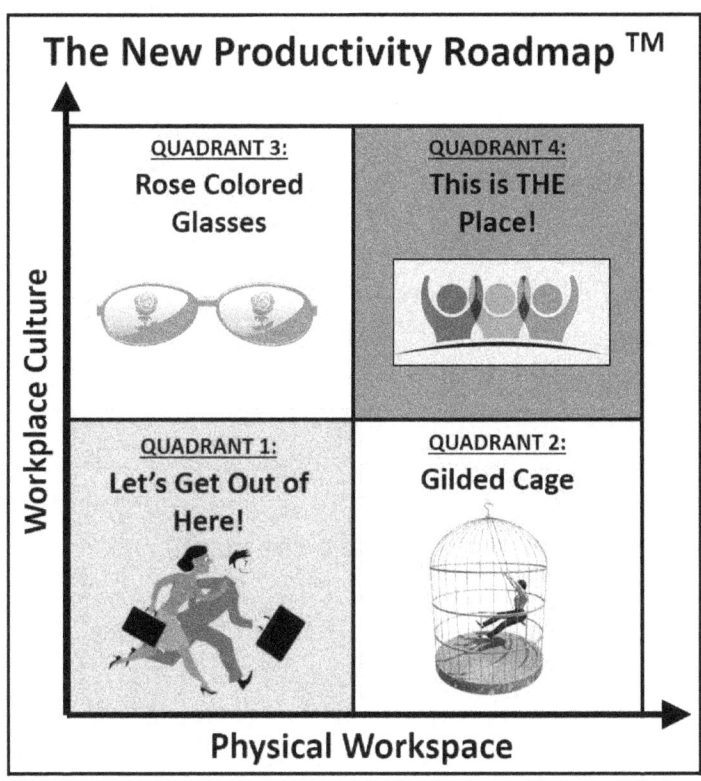

WorkPlaceROI™ maps your workplace conditions into one of the four quadrants, in accordance to the total scores from individual **myPQ™** assessments. the workplace is assigned based. The best workplace conditions are achieved with high scores for both Workplace Culture and the Physical Workspace.

PART 4. THE NEW PRODUCTIVITY ROADMAP

A Reality Check...do these people work for you? A couple of cases based on real work settings.

What About Chilly Carla?

Let's say that Carla works in an air-conditioned building which is overcooled. Some employees find it acceptable, but Carla and most other women find it so uncomfortable that they cannot concentrate. When asked, Carla says she's 20% less productive than when she can work in another building which is warmer. What should leadership do with this information? To the extent that Carla and other employees are correct, how should leaders determine which potential improvement is best? Should they add ceiling fans and make the room warmer? Is it better to just provide logo wear hoodies to those who need them? Or is there a better solution? We can calculate the ROIs of options so that the leadership can make the best decisions based on company, employee and financial data.

PART 4. THE NEW PRODUCTIVITY ROADMAP

The Hi-Tech Team - It's Stuffy in Here

Consider the case of the "Hi-Tech Team". Our surveys with management and employees have indicated that inadequate space ventilation and the resultant stale air were the leading causes of underperforming physical workspace conditions. Technical audits determined that the predicted loss of productivity of $6,500 per employee per year for inadequate ventilation and temperature problems applied to 50% of the workforce. With 50 employees, the expected losses would be $162,500 per year. A preliminary budget for a new central HVAC system (ventilation and AC) for the 11,000 square-foot office space was $230,000. Simple payback of one year and a half is attractive. With longer payback periods we use an NPV (net present value) model to calculate the attractiveness of the investment.

The ability to select between alternatives with individual financial performance (e.g. ROI) puts the leadership in the driver seat to invest wisely and put the money where it creates the greatest value.

"Never neglect details.
When everyone's mind is
dulled or distracted the leader
must be doubly vigilant."

Colin Powell

PART 4. THE NEW PRODUCTIVITY ROADMAP

It's time to ask yourself some important questions

- Do you want to improve productivity by understanding the financial impact of work settings on your organization?
- In the race for engaging and retaining the best of talent in an increasingly competitive market, are you winning?
- Do you need a smooth running and engaged workforce of full-time, part-time and just-in-time contributors?
- Are your leaders prepared to lead in this rapidly changing world of local and global competition?
- Do you worry that the money you spend on employee engagement is not giving you as much ROI as in the early days?
- Are you prepared for a world where most employees expect inclusion and the right to share their individual expectations of the work environment?

Leaders who plan to meet the new expectations of the workforce will succeed in the future – the rest will be in danger of becoming "dinosaurs."

Phyllis Horner, PhD

PART 4. THE NEW PRODUCTIVITY ROADMAP

SUMMARY

We've shown that it's possible to measure employee needs for a productive workplace in a more modern way, that matches what the research says employees expect from their employers today.

We've helped you estimate the cost of inaction for your own productivity, and in estimated losses if your talent leaves you to join a competitor.

Where do you stand right now? How can you find a low-risk way to evaluate the usefulness of this productivity model for your business?

TIME FOR ACTION

1. Review this book with your senior team. (http://amazon.com/author/phyllishorner) Discuss the potential upside of learning more.

2. Contact us for more information. We'd love to hear from you and offer a 30-minute complimentary Zoom consultation.

3. Accept our gift – a complimentary myPQ survey. Go to https://greatplacesandspaces/mypq to claim it today.

"Productivity is never an accident. It is always the result of a commitment to excellence, intelligent planning, and focused effort."

Paul J. Meyer

FINAL THOUGHTS

Now is the very best time to position your organization to win the talent war by taking smart strategic action to bridge the gap between the modern workforce and your current workplace.

Unless you act, your culture increases the risk of fracturing, and you give your competitors a "hunting license" for your talent.

Don't let that happen.

HOW WE HELP COMPANIES AND ORGANIZATIONS

What We Do

The authors, Dr. Phyllis Horner and Dr. Manfred Zapka, experts in their respective fields of productivity /culture and healthy work settings, authored this work to contribute to creating a modern productivity model. Through experience and research, we have built an integrated model, survey and decision tools which help leaders make better choices and "connects the dots" between the physical and "psychological" aspects of work, so that they can be optimally productive, win the "talent wars", and create future success.

Want to Know More? Set an Appointment to Talk with Us

You can reach us at
info@greatplacesandspaces.com

ABOUT THE AUTHORS

Dr. Phyllis Horner and Dr. Manfred Zapka
Founders, Great Places & Spaces LLC

Phyllis Horner, PhD, CEO

Dr. Horner was trained as an I/O Psychologist and has 30 years of workforce planning, talent management, productivity and career systems experience across four states and with solutions for companies from Fortune 5 to 100 people, both public, private, family and not-for-profit. A respected expert on employee productivity, Phyllis is passionate about helping both individuals and companies succeed through workplace design.

She founded Thriving Worklife Design, a coaching and online learning firm dedicated to helping individuals make career changes that match their lives. She helps create a world where work is "not a four-letter word".

ABOUT THE AUTHOR

Manfred Zapka, PhD, PE, LEED AP, WELL AP

Dr. Zapka is a licensed engineer specializing in green and sustainable design for buildings and infrastructure. He is the Healthy Building Expert™ and is a consultant to private and institutional clients. He has taught and conducted research at architecture departments with a focus on high performance buildings and occupant health and comfort. His focus in engineering, teaching and research is the practical application of green buildings and infrastructure so that solutions have a positive financial benefit, in addition to taking care of the health of the people and environment.

www.ingramcontent.com/pod-product-compliance
Lightning Source LLC
Chambersburg PA
CBHW032126090426
42743CB00007B/480